Birth Affirmations

Susan Singer

Published by
Sassy Press
3440 Northridge Road
Richmond, Virginia 23235

www.BirthAffirmationsBook.com

Copyright 2015 by Susan Singer

All rights reserved. With the exception of quoting brief passages for the purposes of review, no part of this publication may be reproduced without prior written permission from the Publisher.

All affirmations in this book are made without any guarantee on the part of the author or Publisher, both of whom also disclaim any liability incurred in connection with the use of these affirmations or specific details.

ISBN: 978-0-9964624-0-2

Printed in the United States of America

Dedicated to the billions of women who have already given birth and to the billions of women who will give birth in the future. You create the human race one precious being at a time.

Foreword

The pregnancy year is transforming and special, but it is also filled with the unknown, the hard and the messy. It can be easy to get caught up in other people's worries, doubts and "horror" stories as well as the dramas in your own life.

The beautifully drawn images in Birth Affirmations are intimate and joyful. The affirmations, simple but ever so true, are serene and soothing. Yet it is the combination of the two that creates the power of this book. What we tell ourselves, what we envision, is important. So often we forget that we have the ability to write the script and create the images that will support us in precisely the way we need. This book is that gentle reminder, the support of what you already know and possess.

As a mother, a birth assistant and an educator, I believe this book is a gift—plain and simple—a gift to all embarking on this sacred and life-altering path of motherhood.

Thérèse Hak-Kuhn
CPBD, CBE and Executive Director of toLabor

Gratitude

Thank you to the women who shared pictures of their most sacred and private moments and allowed me to draw them: Denise, Tina, Mary, Kate, Jacquelyn, Sarah C., Sarah A., Linda, Tracy, Rita, Sue, Evan-Ashley. This book couldn't exist without you.

Thank you to the loving friends who encouraged me throughout this project and supported me by reading drafts of the book, gently suggesting thoughtful changes, encouraging me to continue to improve things, finding typos, and so much more: Tina, Noah, Karen, Shannon, Kathryn, Cindy.

Thank you to my children, Andrew, Laura, and Dylan Kolhoff, who fill my heart with joy every day. Thank you for teaching me about unconditional love, for enabling me to see pure Spirit, and for growing into your fabulous true selves.

Thank you to Nancy Giglio, my midwife, for helping bring Laura and Dylan into the world with such calm, peaceful, loving professionalism. Thank you to all people working to support women in having positive, empowering births.

Thank you to the women in my original women's group who taught me to love being a woman and about sacred birthing: Denise, Cheryl, Anne, Aniela, Mary G., Beth, Mary H., Kirsten. Thank you to Kathy Siegel for giving me my first book of birth affirmations. Thank you to my precious Tina-friend.

Thank you to my husband, Chris Payton, who fills my heart with love and joy and gives me the unconditional support to pursue my myriad creative passions.

Thank you especially to my mother, Emma Lou Marchant Martin, who gave me life and encourages me in all my endeavors.

Susan Singer
June 2015

Introduction

When I was pregnant with my second child, I received a small book of handwritten birth affirmations from a friend. I greedily opened the book and read powerful words that connected me with the universality of birth: "I birth my baby like billions of women before me." "I know how to birth my baby." I breathed in the natural wisdom and beautiful vision contained within that collection. Each day of my pregnancy, I read the words and absorbed them as my own, adding new affirmations as they occurred to me.

The births of all three of my children went smoothly, but the last two, at home, were particularly empowering and wonderful, partially because of the use of these affirmations. The one that resonated most deeply for me was "The pain is my power. It opens me up like a flower in bloom, making room for my baby's entry into the world." When I labored the first time, my Pitocin-induced labor became too much, and I chose to have meds to get through transition. For my second and third births, I chose to perceive the "pain" as the most intense feeling I'd ever experienced and to picture each contraction as my body's way of opening my cervix so my babies could enter the world. These images helped me remain calm and work with the contractions rather than tensing in fear of them. I moved confidently and powerfully through these births and felt completely empowered after birthing my 9 pound, 11 ounce daughter at home and unmedicated. "I am woman, hear me roar!"

Whether you have your baby in the hospital, in a birthing center, at home, or elsewhere, you have the right to choose how you want to birth. May these words help you envision and create the birth that is right for you and all involved.

This book is divided into five sections. The first, My Pregnant Body, celebrates the gloriousness of your new body, your big belly, your fecund shape.

The second section is full of affirmations pertaining to being in labor and giving birth. For some of us, the only births we've seen have been on TV, where the woman suddenly grabs her stomach, leans over, screams, and says, "My water just broke. Take me to the hospital—NOW!" Real births usually proceed very differently from that. These affirmations will help open you up to a more realistic progression of events and are intended to help you cope with and integrate the emotional and physical sensations you may experience.

If you have complications when giving birth or need to have medical intervention, these affirmations can support you in that experience as well: "My baby is safe in God." "My baby finds the perfect position to birth safely, easily, joyfully." There is a great deal of surrender and trust necessary in giving birth. May these affirmations support you in that release. (If the use of the word "God" doesn't work for you, I hope you will easily substitute others which evoke the Great Mystery, All that Is.)

Pregnancy is lengthy, giving us time to adjust to the idea of a baby. Once the baby arrives, reality is sometimes more challenging than our fantasy of how it will be with our precious bundle of joy in our arms. The After Birth affirmations can support you in taking excellent care of yourself and letting yourself be cared for by others as you fulfill this most sacred calling—caring for your baby.

When I was born in 1959, my mother nursed me for about six weeks before societal pressure made it too difficult for her to continue. This is fairly common even today. If you choose to breastfeed your baby, the nursing affirmations will offer you a vision of a lovely, reciprocal relationship that meets both your needs for as long as you and your baby choose to nurse.

The other parts of the book are for you to create. The last page is for you to write your own affirmations as they occur to you. The inside flaps give you space to include pictures of you pregnant and with your baby. The inside cover provides room for your Birth Plan and Birth Story as well as Contact Information for Birth Partners. Feel free to write in the book throughout—it is meant to be a tool, a workbook, a guide, a support, a reminder of just how amazing you are and how perfect the birthing process is, no matter what.

May your pregnancy be full of joyful anticipation and the strength, courage, and grace to get through any rough spots. May your baby's birth be exactly right for all involved. May you trust the process. May your baby bring unconditional love and untold blessings into your life. Should you choose to nurse, may your nursing relationship be uncomplicated and fulfilling. May your new family's life be blessed.

Susan

My Pregnant Body

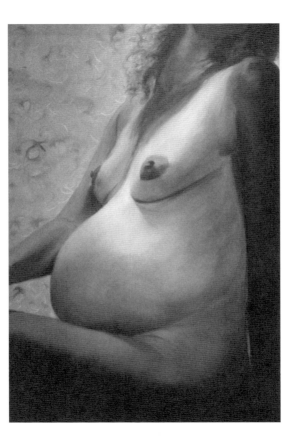

My pregnant body is glorious!

My pregnant body is
strong and powerful and perfect
for birthing my baby.

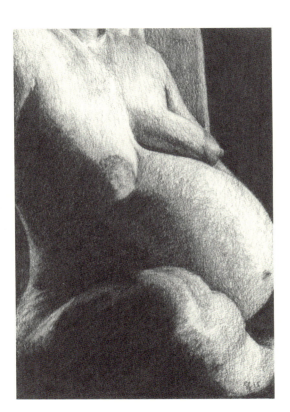

I love my pregnant belly!

I am perfectly designed to birth my baby.

I know how to birth my baby!

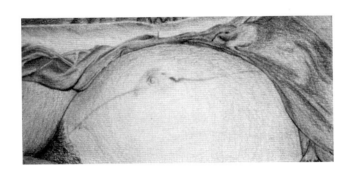

I am wonderfully comfortable
in my luscious body.

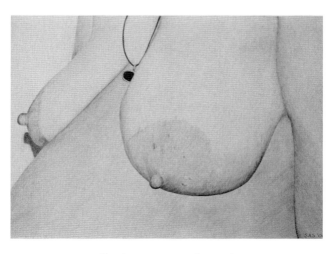

I release my body to do
what it knows how to do naturally.

My belly holds
the mysteries of the Universe within.

My baby is a perfect fit for my body.

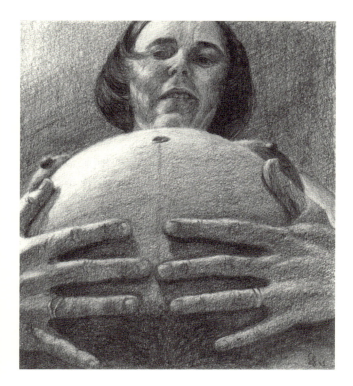

I birth my baby like billions of women before me.

My baby and I deserve
a beautiful and positive birthing experience.

The baby will birth in his or her own perfect time.

I patiently await
my precious baby.

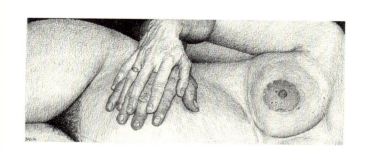

I accept and bless
the path by which this baby comes to us.

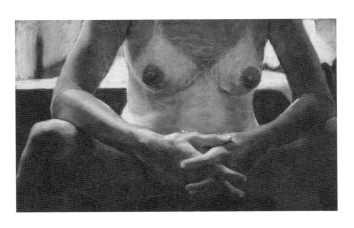

The baby will choose to be born at the perfect time for the baby and all those involved.

Giving Birth

*I birth my baby
beautifully, peacefully, gently, naturally.*

My baby and I are safe in childbirth.

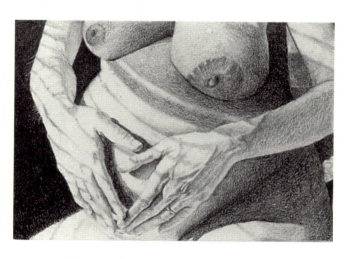

I surrender to the birthing energy—
the Spirit of God moving through me.

I release my body to do the work it needs to do
and knows how to do
to birth the baby.

I know exactly what to do to birth my baby.

My baby finds the perfect position to birth
safely, easily, joyfully.

With each contraction,
my body opens more and more for my baby.

My baby and I
are a perfect match for one another
physically, mentally, spiritually.

My baby and I move and work together
gently and harmoniously,
as our bodies do their miraculous work.

My labor unfolds
and progresses exactly as it should.

The pain is my power.
It opens me up like a flower in bloom,
making room for my baby's entry into the world.

I love my body.

I trust my body.

My body knows how to birth my baby.

It is safe and joyful
to surrender to my birthing energy.

I am safely and joyfully surrendering.

Emotions come and go like the tide.

I can ride the waves.

I will not drown.

My baby comes to me in precisely the right way for all involved.

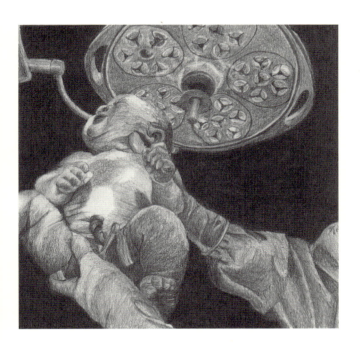

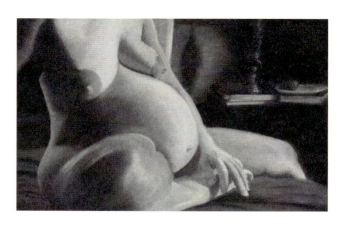

Let go and let God.

The baby is completely safe in God.
I am completely safe in God.

I have all the energy and stamina
I need to birth my baby.

My baby finds the pathway out of my body
and into my arms
safely, easily, peacefully, joyfully.

My body opens easily and
joyfully releases my baby into my arms.

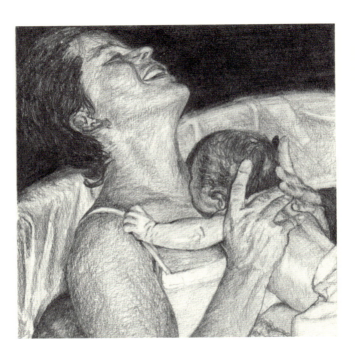

I love my baby.

I open for my baby.

I birth my baby into my arms.

I welcome my baby into the world.

After the Birth

My baby is completely healthy in God.

I have all the energy and stamina I need to care for my baby.

It's OK to rest.

Resting helps me care for my baby better.

It's OK to say NO to visitors.

It's OK to say YES to visitors.

It's OK to ask for help.

Taking care of myself
is the best way to care for my baby.

It's OK to let others care for me while
I care for my baby.

It's not possible to hold my baby too much.

I find comfort in my baby's loving touch.

My baby finds comfort in my loving touch.

I love my baby unconditionally.

My baby loves me unconditionally.

Nursing

I am perfectly equipped to nurse my baby.

Nursing is soothing to both me and my baby.

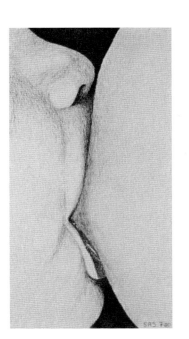

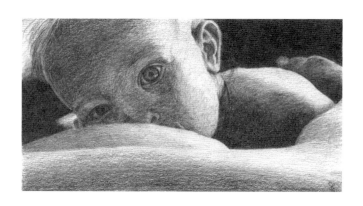

I nurse my baby like billions of women before me.

I love nursing my baby.

Nursing provides the perfect nourishment for my baby.

Nursing my baby is the most natural thing in the world.

Nursing helps my baby flourish.

My milk flows freely to feed my baby.

Nursing helps both me and my baby relax.

My baby and I will know how long to nurse.

My Affirmations